I0015091

Becoming

Becoming

Gray Lee

REDHAWK
PUBLICATIONS

Becoming
Copyright © 2025 Gray Lee

All rights reserved. No part of this publication may be reproduced, distributed, or transmitted in any form or by any means, including photocopying, recording, or other electronic or mechanical methods, without the prior written permission of the publisher, except in the case of brief quotations embodied in critical reviews and certain other noncommercial uses permitted by copyright law. For permission requests, write to the publisher, addressed "Attention: Permissions Coordinator," at the address below.

ISBN: 979-8-89933-003-2 (Paperback)
Library of Congress Control Number: 20250944361

Any references to historical events, real people, or real places are used in a fictitious manner. Names, characters, and places are products of the author's imagination.

Front Cover photo credit: Gray Lee
Author photo credit: Gray Lee
Book design: Robert T Canipe

Printed in the United States of America.

First printing edition 2025

Redhawk Publications
The Catawba Valley Community College Press
2550 Hwy 70 SE
Hickory NC 28602

https://redhawkpublications

For Scott,

Who left a note

In a book not so

long ago to know

that I am not alone.

Table of Contents

Just So You Know…

My words do not come gently, but claw

From the corners of my mind, tearing

Muscle and flesh to shreds till

My thoughts bleed thick syrup

From my eyes,

        From my mouth,

          From my nose,

Onto the torn-out parchment,

        The margins of books,

          The backs of pictures.

My words stain all that I touch.

Nature's Tomb

Oh, my Ophelia,

    Madness rushes like water

    Winding through the streams

    Who know you so well,

    Thick with familial blood.

      He twisted the knife.

Sad eyed Ophelia,

    Bare your neck to the sun,

    He has no use for your sanity.

    The babbling of this brook

    Will carry you gently downstream.

    Drift entwined with the branch

    Snapped like your strained lucidity

    As bosom blossoms to lilies.

      Feel its presence.

      Cradle its soul.

      For now it rocks

      Your sun kissed corpse

      Like a sleeping infant

      In her mother's arms.

I Dreamt My Blood Was Honey

Pooling in my chest,
Slow beat spreading golden
Syrup clogging my arteries,
Weighing down my limbs
Like freshly poured cement.

It leaks from my eyes,
Nose, ears, mouth.
Sticky tears smell so sweet
Even to bears and bees,
Swarming my face,
To devour my candied flesh.

Sickly saccharine suffocation,
Brilliant sugary death,
When knees hit the ground
And worlds begin to tilt,
Blurring edges sunny gold,
Consuming vision and thought.

A Bite

I feel as if I
Might take a bite out of life
Hold veins in my teeth
And taste the iron tang of
Experience on my tongue.

Field of Lilies

They smell of cherries and cigarettes.

An odd combination

Seeing that they don't smoke,

But they always take the

Cherries off my milkshake,

Trying to tie a knot with their tongue.

They look like sin,

But the gentlest of sins:

Poison in a pastry,

A dagger dressed in flowers.

Their hands, soft yet deadly.

Their lips spit venom

Yet soothe my soul.

They hold me in their arms

And whisper through cold air.

But as quickly as they were here,

They disappeared.

Monster

There is this monster above me.

It's rugged paws on my shoulders,

Pungent breath down my neck,

As blood drips from its voracious maw

Into my thinning and matted hair.

The stench forces silence down my throat,

Gagging on its way down.

I reach up my hands before the beast,

Hoping for an attack to tame my anguish

But am met with only my own trembling fingers

Hovering before my own blood-soaked mouth

Still choking from biting my own tongue.

Eve

I was brought here in pain.
Split in two, I cried out in agony
Against this first act of loncliness.

I wandered.

I took his fruit, ate of it greedily,
But stole nothing of his virtue.
That was always given freely.

I was blamed.

Scorn me to crawl on my raw belly.
Crush my neck under your heel
And call me beautiful.

I bear your sons, you cast me out.
I roam here, with him, for years
Just to be taken by another.

Throw me to the dogs after you're through.
Leave my weathered body on this doorstep.

Ichor runs under this skin
But bleeds red the same
So, they go on cutting,
Dissecting, limb from limb.
Twelve pieces for your tribes
After a night where the moon
Drags sorrowful across the sky.

Make me but your warning,
Your battle cry.

Creation Story

In the beginning, God didn't create shit.

He didn't rip the veil between night and day.

He didn't dump out the ocean and lift up the clouds.

He didn't raise the lands and dig out the caverns.

He didn't kiss the Earth with saccharine fruits.

He didn't breathe life to Adam or break ribs for woman.

Adam was not gifted a garden, but he toiled for one.

He spent years surviving,

      Evolving,

          Thriving,

To reach that garden; and once he found paradise,

He destroyed it,

leaving only ashes behind.

God didn't create shit, but if he did-

If he ripped the veil,

      Raised the lands,

          Kissed the Earth,

He made a mistake.

He made man.

He made shit.

To Write

Pencil gripped as my
Soul pours from every orifice
Of my being.

Morbidly Holy

Churches are beautiful places.
The worn oak pews, perfectly
symmetrical in uniform rows.
Three columns, separated by carpet isles.
Sunlight filters through aged stained glass,
painting the sanctuary in hues of
green and blue, red and pink.
The windows hold stories of
creation and rolling fields,
archangels and rebirth.
One candle still flickers with life
on the altar, never burning out.
The flame casts an eerie shadow,
reflecting off the golden olive branch
grasped tight in the beak of a dove.
As the bells sing out for noon,
the sun bursts through the skylight,
bathing the son in light and
reflecting off his cloak of white.
A warm halo encircles his head
as his walnut body sparkles in the light,
But the sun cannot reach the crevices
of his ebony wood grained body.
His smile painted with golden rays
still hides cool sawdust untouched
by the father's bright light, somehow
both welcomed and shunned to dark corners.

This is his house
and I am a trespasser.

His eyes burn through my chest,
saints surrounding mock
my clasped hands to my breast.
These colors seem dimmer in the shadows,
this candle burns a little lower.
His words become distorted
through the mouth of the grandiose
of golden pulpits and purple robes.
This place used to be so welcoming,
so holy and divine, but now I stand
enveloped in its morbid beauty
And shiver under his gaze.

The Endless Suffering of Abel

I tried to write of beauty
But Abel's blood cried out to me
His screams pierced my ears
Till my own blood ran down my neck
And mingled with his innocence
It fills the groves of my fingertips
Guilty thumbprints mark the path
Of the centuries of his torment

As I trudge through this valley
I drag his corpse behind me
From Pennsylvania Avenue
To the prisons of El Salvador
He screams out their names
Into the echoed halls
Of his concrete cages

His bony fingers wrap around my ankles
Crawling through mud paths carved
By a hundred thousand pairs of feet
Who shouldered his burden
From my home to Oklahoma

Across continents I hear him
He paints the cities red
From the borders of Ukraine
To the streets of Gaza
His voice carried through
The laughs and cries
Of children's eyes

Cain became the first to draw blood
But we painted it across the land
And when his voice asks me, I answer:
Am I not my brother's keeper?

Why Write of God?

Because I too am a myth.
A pillar of fire to pierce the night.
Egypt's Exodus.

I am but a swarm of locust
Buzzing eardrums to burst
And peeling back boils
Oozing infection onto delicate skin.

I am a lie, supernatural in origin.
Oral traditions, faded parchment.
A mighty son, both god and man.
A child of cherubs capable of both
Life and destruction.

I am both the angel
And his fiery sword.

Whisper my ninety-nine names.
Tremble at my word.
I stand here with this deity
Who knows not my name.
One foot in glory,
The other in the grave.

Why Write of God? (Pt. 2)

Because I too am real.
Hands of flesh and bone.
Bleeding skin.

I am the cherubim morning star
With my four faces turning.
Seasons changing and trapped
In the ox, human, lion, and eagle.

I am comfort with a thousand titles.
Ancient stories, dead languages.
A human boy, but God or Man?
A whisper of hope as broad
As my outstretched arms.

I am not the word,
But an all-encompassing voice.

Cry out my ninety-nine names
And every name they do not claim
I stand here surrounded
By unexplainable raging beauty
My feet planted in glory:
Same clay as my grave.

At Seven

I am not a poet
I might be
A storyteller
A compulsive liar
Outspoken always
Hotheaded
All calloused
Feet and hands
Bloody knuckles
Big smiles and
Bigger laughs
I bare my teeth
Stomp my heels in
To the sandaled toes
Of a taunting voice

I hoot and howl
Bamboo staff
Tied to my waist
And we fence
Till our hands are
Filled with splinters
And our ribs
Colored purple

I growl guttural

Gurgling tears
In my throat and
Bite back hard
At the hand that
Points and laughs

One day my parents
Got a call from school
After a boy pinned me
To the playground fence
With a briar branch
Clutched in my
Trembling fist
I cut his face but
I cut my hands too

First Encounters

I can't remember the first time I experienced sexism

    Maybe it was when I was six

    And the little boy in my class told me

    My clothes weren't "girly" enough

    Maybe it was when his mother backed him up

    Told my mother she should buy me a dress

        "Just not to confuse the other children"

It could have been when I was eight

    And the teacher told me I talk too much

    But never scolded the boy I spoke to

    As he reached forward and pulled on my pigtails

        "He just has a crush on you, ignore him"

Perhaps it was when I was eleven

    And my father told me not to wear leggings

        "They just make you look easy"

    I didn't understand what he meant

Or maybe it was when I was thirteen

    And the boy I had trusted since the first grade

    Struck his hand on my cheek

    That led me to the floor

        The entire room was watching

        But no one said a word

It could have been when I was sixteen

    On that mission trip with a youth family

    And the mother sat me down to tell me

    I would one day have a husband and children

"You were born to care for a family"

She made me feel guilty

For never wanting a child of my own

But I think it might have been the moment I was born

When they placed a pink beanie on my head

A hat that never seemed to fit right

And christened me pretty and soft

Before I learned to say my own name.

Pygmalion's Wife

He willed me into existence
Forged me from his desire,
Molded me to his image.
He spun my hair from threads
Of his own rotted disappointment.
His stench like dying lilies
Consumes my senses.

No woman will ever be enough
But I am no woman,
For my skin is alabaster.

Disgust drenches his clothes
But seeps in awe through my skin.
Defiled in thought, too perfect
A beauty to grace the Earth,
He took my hand before it was flesh.
He promised me life, but only
To dissolve in his shadow.

Bathe me in your gaze
Is that not why I was made?
Undress me with your eyes,
Dine upon these thighs,
Kiss my marble lips
With your grim and wilted petals.
I am but a sculpture's bride.
I am woman, but still
A statue in his Bath.

Clay

Cut me to pieces
Tear away my edges
Mold me into who
You know I could be
Pull at the strings
Of my taut heart
Twist my words to
Accompany your song
Make me into
What you desire
I can be anything
You could ever want
Just don't leave me
Behind when you
Grow bored of me

Your Feast

Soothed to submission
I could feel the knife split
Me from chin to flank
You worked my innards loose, slipped
Soul from ribcage, mind from body

Now, swiftly with strong hands
You carve between my ribs
Clean through fifth and sixth
And sliced through my sternum

With feather soft touch
Cut through my abdomen, then trace
Your fingertips down my spine
Lift my breasts from my chest
And splice my back into racks

Cut loin from saddle
And hips from thighs
Kiss my navel before
You dig into my side
Bleed me dry
I am your sacrifice

An Elegy

For Hunter. I can never forget you.

On the far side of midnight, I find
You, with your dark curls and bright eyes
You, with gap teeth and cracked lips, hidden
Inside my treehouse with a staff at your side
You, with hands as rough as mine, always
Cradling your bleeding, exposed heart

On the far side of midnight, your face
Seems to shine like starlight, distorted
By the fading lucidity of exhaustion
You, perpetually fifteen, frozen in time
And I imagine your face, aged like mine

Tomorrow is your birthday, but I will celebrate
Alone, each year as the clock
Turns to the far side of midnight

Clover

I remember your lips –
Pale pink; flowers chained,
Blushing against dark curls,
And gap teeth giddy
Under summer's gentle gaze.

I remember red crowns –
Brilliant gold showers in the wood
Where we hide in hollow trees
Closed eyes to the chill
That hides behind walls.

I finally came to you in snow
With pink petals gripped
In frost-bitten fingers
To lay across a stone.
Bearing weight of solemn snow,
Mittens wipe clean the etched stone
That speaks of a summer clover
Surrendered to the cold.

My Father is Made of Smoke

His stench hovers stale
In the air; he rises up
From neighborhood bonfires
In the heavy summer fever

He tumbles towards the trees
Escaping from his mouth
After a long, burning drag
Cigarette or spliff

He passes to my hands,
Stains my fingers black
Eyes trained on my face
As I breathe in his presence

He burns holes in my lungs
When I slowly exhale
His silent stare
Flicks ash on my arms

We sit on this rotting porch
And watch the sunset
As my father slowly drifts
From the fire he lit

Walk With My Mother

As the daisies bloom
And the blackberries ripen
The summer sun will melt my neurons
Into a kaleidoscope of colors
Flashing like aster in the field

The basking lizard calls me
To bathe in your gaze
Here to let it fill me
To the brim and overflow
I feel myself spill out
Down the rolling hills
To meet her along the way
To wander beside streams

I commune with her here
Along worn dirt roads
And barbed wire fences
Where I walk with her breath
Whispered through the trees
To bloom in her brightness
And overflow with her waters
That baptize me again
And blanket me in her breath

Deerfield

Walking down these dirt roads
Lined tires stacked to a fence,
A hawk screeches.

He circles high before landing
On a barren bough; heavy
Wings spread then tucked.
He stands guard, stoic
With nothing left to protect.

As the sun sets, he watches
Whitetails take over the valley,
Swarming from patchy forests
Littered with the rotting corpses
Of clear-cut abandoned pines.

They rule this valley at dusk
With their warily quick feet,
Dancing over the fields in droves,
And overrun this valley by dawn.

From his watchtower, the hawk dives,
Gliding over antlers and spotted fawns.
He lands once again at the foot of a doe.
Her wet nose leans in for a better look,
Bowing to this feathered vision.

Source of life; guardian blest;
Yet an absence between.
A bond been broken.
The rope that binds them
Severed generations ago.

Baptism

Upon this hill stands a house
With rocking chairs older than the foundation
And a kerosene lamp still left on the bedside table.
The rush of the river drowns out passing cars,
Calling me to its creeks that run behind
The rotting garden shed where she so tenderly cared for lilies.
Prayers are spoken around an old oak table,
But we rush out the screened door,
Shoving each other to the grass, tumbling
Towards the muddy riverbank.
We sink our toes into frigid water,
Hopping along rocks and yelling to passing snakes,
Laughing as their slender bodies cut swift through the current.
Mud pies and watermelon stain our round cheeks
And with grimy sugar caked to our clothes,
We let the waterfall baptize us again
In the name of salamanders, streams,
And sweet Appalachian air
Before she calls us back home over the grassy knoll.

Gaia

Blessed at birth by
Holy hands; Gift
To plant seeds, grow
Life; Bear fruit trees
On strong hips and
Pass wisdom of willows
To saplings and seeds.
With mud brown feet
And sun-soaked skin,
The grounding of the mind,
Soul and body entwined.
A rain of quiet solidarity
Quenches thirst of tyranny
Like milk offerings for the
Ichor brimmed Goddess.

Hurricane

For Western North Carolina.

I have been here before in a dream–
The wind caresses the willow trees. My grandmother
in her rocking chair, scrapes along the rotted floorboards.
Bright candles peek through quilted curtains to wave
at passing ghosts who wander these ancient woods.
Her songs rise from the stream that runs behind, calling me
to the rocky banks to commune here. Her words wrap
around my ankles in the frigid water and mingle
with her stories of sweet Appalachian air.

   Her voice rages now.

   Disfigured in the deluge of rain.

The water reshaped her into a river and
whisked her down the mountain till she crashed
through her rotted porch, splintered oak embedded in her skin
and broken glass graced her sunken face as she overflowed
out the paned windows. Rushing along roads, she pillaged.
Stole memory boxes carved with bobcats and white tails.
She carried her bottle trees downstream and piled them
at my doorstep before she threw herself
across the threshold and she spilled out onto the floor.

   She ruined my carpet.

   She broke my window.

She whipped through the tall pines and leapt
across power lines till they toppled like dominoes
along the road, fragmented asphalt piled to stairs in her wake.
Her panicked, strained arms grabbed helplessly
for what they could in hopes to anchor her here, but
instead, she buries them beneath her harshly.
Bloated bodies line her path where the river reveals her sins.
Once the water subsides, their stench still fills my nostrils
as it mixes with honeysuckle and gardenias.

      She destroyed my garden.

      She ravaged my city.

But her waters receded when her rage was spent
and the mountains forgave her, let her gather herself up
and crawl back to her fallen home whose walls could no longer
hold her despair which she let flood the tributaries and streams.
The windows too broken to hang a quilted curtain and the roof
too absent to save her from herself, so she now sits
on what remains of her rotted porch and waits for the waves

      To wash her downstream

      To flood my doorstep again.

For David

From the perspective of Jonathan, son of Saul, next in line for the king-dom of Israel.

My beautiful Most Beloved,
From the moment I laid eyes on you
my soul was knit to yours.
Favored first by God and then
my father, till he favored hate.
He tried to take you from this life
more times than I care to remember, placed
You in his armor to face the giant,
great Philistine you slayed with stone.

You needed no armor.
Your courage was enough.

So, you shed it like the shame you told me
I mustn't hold on to in your presence.
You had no use for self-hatred
but you carried mine gladly.
I dressed you in my robes, sweet tanned
limbs untouched by battle like smooth
olive oil butter and we danced
on the mountain, made a vow sealed with a kiss
that I'd protect you always, aid you
in your escape from my father's madness
when that evil spirit took hold of him.

I prayed your sinful perfection might
never abandon me or this world.

I signaled your safe departure
with far off arrows. You bowed
three divine times with your lips
to the cracked dusty ground.
I wished they had kissed my own.

You departed in a flurry of tears
and promises we could not keep,
for I knew I would not see you again.
For your sake or for mine, I did not know.

With my father and brothers,
I was slain on that mountaintop
where I first dressed you in my robes
and bequeathed to you my throne.
Now, even as my bleeding body is dragged to
caves where I will be anointed once again,
I still love you as I love my own being.
I will watch as you carry on without me, caring
for my crippled son, and let him sit beside
you at what used to be our table.

Breaking of Bread

A crowded, damp basement
Where archangels dance–
Matted halo on your brow
Strobed wings, pale skin
Sweat like ichor down arms
And rosary 'round your neck
It tangles in my fingers
Begging for a prayer
Ten "hail Mary"s
For a taste of communion.
"Take and eat
This is my body"

Now fallen to my knees
Spill pleas of forgiveness
My quiet psalms of praise
Till bread meets lips
With simple holy sighs
Like wine on my tongue
Or manna gifts from God

Metamorphosis

Wake here, with me
Duvet stuffed to the foot,
Sheets over her head.
She sleeps a few more hours
So, I watch her breathe
As the sun peaks through the blinds
Over the barren, shaking trees.

Eyes burn crown, nape, spine
Shoulder slip, palms open
Accept this, my being
And unveil the lamb on her altar.
She opens her blouse and
Monarchs beat wings on breasts.

To the ceiling, along walls
She flutters to glassy panes.
Pale light passes through veins
Of brilliant orange and gold
Cast her colors on my face
And memorize her pattern
As she disappears through
The still open window.

La Petite Mort

I feel it building,
Boiling under my ribs,
Pushing up my throat, trying to escape
Through my shredded vocal cords,
Peeling the skin back on my face.

I want to peel back your dress.
Sink my claws into something sweet,
Maim it.

Rip your supple skin and hold
Your jugular delicately between my teeth.
I'll end you with this little death
As you drain the heat from my soul.

But my lips still crave the penny taste
Of blood and you are not here.
So, I'll rip at my own weathered skin,
Sink my claws into my own rotted flesh,
And cry out in agony at my own little death.

Only to find this hunger
That still rages within me.
Only you could be enough to quench it.

Sting

Where her hollow smiles
Hold venomous wasps who don't
Sting without regret

Becoming

Who am I?
I can tell you who I'm not:
I am not my mother's daughter
Else my skin wouldn't crawl
When she calls me "young woman"

I am not my father's son
Else my arms would be able
To carry the weight of
His father and his before him

I am not their Christian child
Even as I fall to my knees
With my tear-stained cheeks
Praying to a God whose hand
Has not reached down to us
In thousands of years.

I am not truthful
As lies spill from my mouth,
Weaving the web of my mind
Into a knot impossible to untangle
Morphing fact and fable
Till I cannot even tell the difference.

You ask me who I am
But I sit mute with no answer.
How can I know who I am
When all I have ever done is
Pretend to be something I'm not?

Acknowledgments

First, I would like to thank Patty Thompson and the Red-hawk Publications team for providing me with this opportunity to publish my work with them. Redhawk has helped me learn a great deal about the publishing process, as well as helped me get my foot in the door in the publishing and editing world. Without them, this chapbook would never have been possible.

I would also like to thank my outstanding professors at Lenoir-Rhyne University, who helped me grow in my writing skills across the fields of poetry, fiction, and technical writing—specifically Scott Owens, Dale Bailey, and Jennifer Heller. Each of these instructors has helped me improve in ways I never imagined and has given me confidence in myself as a writer.

Lastly, I want to thank my friends and family who have stood by me and encouraged me to follow my heart and pursue writing: my parents, Donna and Wade Lee, for their endless support; my grandparents, Annie and Gil Brauch, for their love and financial support in my college career and personal writing endeavors; and finally, my wonderful partner, Ingrid Kurtz, who has done nothing but love and support me through this process, reading my poetry even though she claims that "poetry isn't her strong suit."

Thank you so much to these individuals—and all the others I may have forgotten to mention—for believing in me!

About the Author

Gray Lee (that's me!) is an English and Creative Writing student at Lenoir-Rhyne University who was given the opportunity to intern for Redhawk Publications, leading to the publication of *Becoming*, their first poetry collection. Born and raised in Hickory, North Carolina, Gray has spent a lot of time exploring the local art and literature scene, using the poetry and coffee HQ of Tasteful Beans Coffee Shop as their writing haven to complete many of their poems and short stories. When not basking in the sun at the outdoor coffeehouse seating, Gray can be found walking the local parks with their dog, Bowie. (Yes, he is named after the singer; Yes, I also have a Bowie tattoo; And yes, I am aware my obsession is a little concerning.) As a queer poet from Appalachia, Gray often writes about the nature and religious ideals they were surrounded by and the impacts that had on their identity, expression, and experiences, which they hope can help connect and inspire other upcoming writers and queer kids who feel lost in what can be such an isolating place—showing them that yes, we exist here too, and yes, we can thrive here as well.

www.ingramcontent.com/pod-product-compliance
Lightning Source LLC
Chambersburg PA
CBHW031601060326
40783CB00026B/4180